HEALTHY·LIVING·

Talking About

The Dangers of Taking Risks

Clifton Park - Halfmoon Public Library
475 Moe Road
Clifton Park, New York 12065

**By Hazel Edwards
and Goldie Alexander**

Gareth Stevens
Publishing

Please visit our Web site **www.garethstevens.com**. For a free color catalog of all our high-quality books, call toll free 1-800-542-2595 or fax 1-877-542-2596.

Library of Congress Cataloging-in-Publication Data

Edwards, Hazel.
Talking about the dangers of taking risks / Hazel Edwards and Goldie Alexander.
    p. cm. — (Healthy living)
Includes index.
ISBN 978-1-4339-3659-3 (library binding)
1. Health behavior in children—Juvenile literature. 2. Risk-taking (Psychology) in children—Juvenile literature. I. Alexander, Goldie, 1936- II. Title.
RJ47.53.E39 2010
613'.0433—dc22

                    2009043440

Published in 2010 by

Gareth Stevens Publishing

111 East 14th Street, Suite 349

New York, NY 10003

For Gareth Stevens Publishing:

Art Direction: Haley Harasymiw

Editorial Direction: Kerri O'Donnell

Cover photo: iStockphoto

Photos and illustrations:

iStockphoto, pages 5–23, 25–30; Newspix, page 20; Photos.com, page 4; UC Publishing, pages 10–11, and 24.

4941

Printed in the United States of America

CPSIA compliance information: Batch #CW10GS: For further information contact Gareth Stevens, New York, New York, at 1-800-542-2595.

Contents

What is risky business?

Every time you plan to do something, you take a risk. Things might not work out. There is always a chance that something may change—the weather, your health, your responsibilities, your situation. It is possible that you could be hurt or upset. You can't control the world, but that shouldn't stop you from planning a picnic, crossing a street, or going away from your home where you feel safe. Risk taking is a normal part of everyday life. It can be positive and good. If you did not take risks, you would never try anything new. But taking risks that you have thought about is different from doing something without taking proper care.

What are unhealthy risks?

When you behave in a way that could harm you or could put others in danger, you are taking unhealthy risks. Laws have been made to protect people from some harmful risks. It is illegal for children to drink alcohol, drive a car, be a passenger without a seatbelt, and buy cigarettes. For many other of life's risks, it is up to you to make the best choices and act in a safe way.

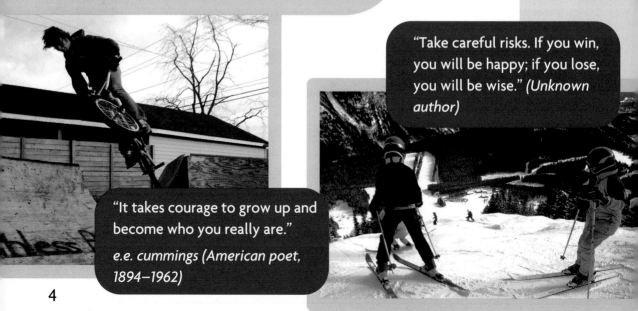

"Take careful risks. If you win, you will be happy; if you lose, you will be wise." *(Unknown author)*

"It takes courage to grow up and become who you really are."

e.e. cummings (American poet, 1894–1962)

Are you a risk taker?

If you've been riding BMX bikes for years, your idea of what is risky will be different from someone who is just starting out in the sport. Your experiences of life with your family and friends have a big impact on what you see as safe or dangerous. Try this quiz to see how much of a risk taker you are.

Give the actions listed below a rating on the Risk Meter. When you have finished, talk about your answers with someone else. Do you agree about what is safe, risky, and dangerous? If not, why might that be so?

- taking something from someone's schoolbag without asking
- walking alone to a friend's house for lunch
- flying overseas for a holiday
- doing research on the Internet for a project
- taking medicine that was meant for someone else
- riding a skateboard without a helmet
- taking something from a shop without paying for it
- chopping the vegetables to make soup
- being a passenger in a car
- spending time in the sun without wearing sunscreen
- getting into the car of somebody you do not know

5 = clearly dangerous stuff

4 = becoming dangerous stuff

3 = definitely risky business

2 = just a little bit risky

1 = safe; not risky at all

Risk Meter

Why do people take risks?

Just as we all come from different families and backgrounds, we also have different reasons for taking risks—even unhealthy risks. Here are a few of the common ones.

Some people are naturally more confident and adventurous than others. They like to experiment. They enjoy the sense of excitement they feel when doing something different, new, or challenging. Bold people like to take risks for fun.

Sometimes people who are unhappy or confused take risks as a way of escaping their problems. They might put themselves in dangerous situations because they do not see themselves as valuable and important people. They need help. Their risk taking is a way of asking others to notice and help them.

Sometimes you might want to do the opposite of what you have been told to do. You are disobedient on purpose, just to prove that you can act independently.

Wanting to belong to a group or be accepted by someone you admire might lead you to do things you might not usually do. You might show off to impress somebody or take an unhealthy risk as a dare to try to get someone to like you.

Sometimes people just do things on the spur of the moment. Have you ever been part of a conversation like this one?

I sort of knew from the moment I did it that it wasn't smart. I just couldn't stop myself. Now here I was, face-to-face with two really unhappy parents!

"What were you thinking, James?"

Dad was not angry, but his jaw was clenched. That's the way it always is when he's trying hard not to raise his voice. And Mom was sitting perfectly still and quiet. I thought she might be about to cry. I gulped.

"Well?" Dad continued. "Can you just help me to understand what went through your mind? Because I have to tell you, James, it's a mystery to me."

What could I say to make it better? What could I say at all? There was nothing else I could do but tell the truth and own up.

"To be honest, Dad, I wasn't thinking at all. I just did it."

"Do you think that's a good enough reason, James?"

"No. I know it's not good enough, Dad, but it's true. I'm sorry. It was dumb. I know that now. But at the time, I just didn't think at all."

"That's disappointing, to say the least. We expect better from you, but thank you for owning up. Next time, use your brain. You're a smart person who just did a very silly thing. Now, go to your room and see if you can work out how you can make up for it."

7

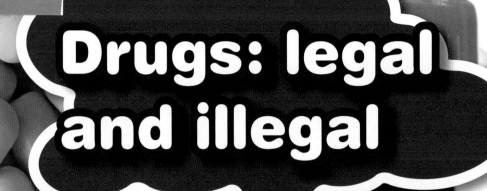

Drugs: legal and illegal

What is a drug?

A drug is a substance that affects the way your mind and/or your body acts. It can be a powder, a liquid, a gas, or a solid. A drug is usually a mixture of chemicals that you put into your body to alter how your body feels or works. This might be to:

• relieve the discomfort of being sick or injured

• cure a disease or condition

• prevent something from happening (the way some shots protect you from catching a disease).

A drug will not affect everybody the same way. What cures one person might make another person ill. Different amounts, or doses, of a drug are needed by different people. Doctors must decide what drugs people need and in what amounts. They **prescribe** the drugs their patients need.

> The law allows the use of some drugs (legal drugs). Other drugs are not permitted by law (illegal drugs).

Occasionally, a person may take certain drugs for a long time (even under the care of the doctor) and become **addicted** to them. Sleeping pills and painkillers, for example, can be addictive.

When is a legal drug illegal?

Although a drug may be legal for one person, it can be illegal for someone else to use that drug if it hasn't been prescribed for them. A drug becomes illegal when:

- the wrong person uses it;
- it is used in the wrong dosage;
- (in certain countries) it is transported across the border;
- it is sold by someone who does not have official permission to sell drugs.

Which drugs are legal?

Only drugs listed as legal within a country and prescribed by doctors are legal.

What about coffee, alcohol, and tobacco?

Because alcohol, tobacco, and the caffeine that is found in coffee affect the way your body works, they can be called drugs. Laws control how old you have to be before you make the decision to use alcohol or tobacco. After that, people can decide for themselves how much to use and how often. There are no laws about using caffeine.

Which drugs are illegal?

Illegal drugs are drugs that have not been prescribed by a doctor or made up and sold by a proper **pharmacist**. Illegal drugs are not on the list of drugs doctors are allowed to prescribe. They are usually taken by people who want to feel happy or who are looking for a thrill, not by sick people wanting to feel well.

Illegal drugs are seriously dangerous business.

Prescriptions: at the pharmacy

What's a prescription drug?

Medicines for some common health problems like headaches, colds, and rashes can be bought at a **pharmacy** or even at the supermarket. These are called over-the-counter drugs and can be bought by any adult. Families often keep such drugs at home in case of sickness or injury.

Sometimes, after figuring out what is wrong, a doctor might write a prescription (also called a script) for a suitable medicine or drug. These special drugs are meant only for the person who is ill and nobody else. Prescription drugs can help the person who is sick but can harm, or even kill, anyone else. They must be handled carefully and responsibly.

Prescription drugs can only be supplied by a health-care professional—an expert. The pharmacist is a health-care professional. The pharmacist makes up the prescription very carefully for the patient. Let's look at what happens at the pharmacy.

This pharmacy sells makeup, gifts, perfumes, and diapers, as well as medicines.

At local pharmacies, people often ask what to buy for minor health problems or what to do if their baby is crying at night. Pharmacists can only make general comments and tell them to see a doctor if the problem continues.

Doctors write the prescriptions and, when patients bring them in, pharmacists have to **dispense** or make up what is required. Pharmacists check up on the doctor's details to make sure the prescription is real.

Pharmacists keep very careful records, especially of dangerous drugs called controlled substances. All pills have to be accounted for. Often a pharmacist has stores of valuable drugs and these must be kept in a locked cabinet.

Pharmacists type the labels with instructions about dosage (how much) and frequency (how often). They also explain what the doctor has instructed.

Healthy people also use pharmacies. For example, they might come in with things like prescriptions for travel drugs.

Pharmacists have to keep professional secrets. They cannot talk to people about prescriptions they have made up for others.

Read the label

Labeling in the past

"Step right up! Step right up! What I have here for you, ladies and gentlemen, will amaze and enthrall. Paddy's Perfect Polypopable Potion will change your life. Losing your hair? Not a problem! Rub some potion on your head each night and you'll have lovely locks forever. Need to lose weight? Easy. Just one spoonful in a glass of water for breakfast and dinner each day, and you will soon see your waistline shrink. Feeling poorly? Polypopable Potion will pick you up. Get your bottle here today. Step right up! Step right up!"

In the 1800s, there were no laws about labeling drugs with information about their contents. Salesmen could make up their own recipes and sell their potions at markets and traveling sideshows. People had no way of knowing what the potions actually contained. Sometimes, the bottles contained nothing more than colored water. Sometimes, the potions had poisons in them. Sometimes, people would take extra doses, thinking that if one sip would make them feel better, two sips would make them feel twice as good. Today, there are laws to stop this from happening.

Some drugs can poison you or cause a bad reaction, such as a rash or vomiting. You need good information when you buy:

- prescription drugs;
- medicines available without a prescription (over-the-counter drugs);
- sunscreen;
- vitamins.

What's so special about the label?

The label tells you what you are buying, what the drug can do for you, and how to use it. It also gives other information.

Storage: Where to keep the drug stored. Some drugs need to be kept in the fridge or at a special temperature.

Expiration date: When the drug must be used by.

Batch number, company name and address: Exactly when the drug was made and by whom. This may be needed if there is a problem with the drug.

Always read the labels on medicines.

 Check to see if it is registered in your country.

 Check the uses to make sure they are suitable for your needs.

 Read all directions and warnings carefully. Always follow them.

 Check the storage conditions, including the recommended temperature. Ensure all medications are kept out of reach of small children.

 Check the expiration date. When the date is reached, safely dispose of any remaining medicine or return it to the pharmacy where you purchased it.

 See if the batch number and supplier's name and address are visible.

Risky stuff at home

We usually think of our homes as safe places, but homes can house some pretty risky things. We need to stop and think about how we can make our home truly safe.

Safety quiz

Which of the things listed below should be kept in a basic **first-aid** kit?

- safety pins
- notepad and pencil
- scissors
- tape
- plastic bags
- **antiseptic**
- bandages
- tweezers
- disposable gloves
- clip seal
- saline solution
- face shield

If you said that ALL those things should be there, give yourself a pat on the back. But do you know what they are all for? Go to *www.mayoclinic.com/health/ FirstAidIndex/FirstAidIndex* and *kidshealth. org/parent/firstaid_safe/* for reliable information.

Are these things poisonous?

- kitty litter
- shoe polish
- perfume
- liquid soap
- furniture polish
- potting mix
- gasoline
- cough medicine
- paint
- drain cleaner
- shaving cream
- bubble mixture

Yes, they *all* are. Everything on the list could be poisonous if swallowed, especially by children. That's why it is important to store drugs and poisons where they can only be reached by adults. A locked medicine cabinet is a good idea. If someone in your family swallows something dangerous, spills poison on their skin, or sprays it into their eyes, you can call the Poison Control Center at 1-800-222-1222.

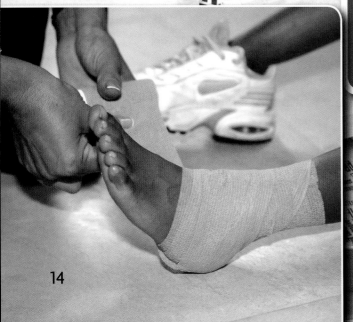

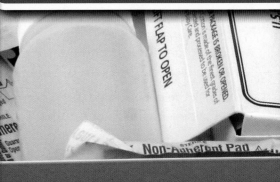

Are these statements true or false?

A. There's a wealth of great information on the Internet.

B. It's safe to chat to anyone on the Internet.

C. Bullying only happens on the playground.

D. Nothing on the Internet is truly private.

A. True. The Internet is like having an enormous library in the computer. However, not all the information found on the Internet is correct.

B. False. Talking to strangers on the Internet is just as dangerous as talking to strangers in person. Take care. People can pretend to be anyone on the Internet.

C. False. Online bullies can invade your home via your computer or mobile phone.

D. True. You should never give out personal and private information. Even your password and log-in name should not give away who you are.

Find out more about Internet safety at
kidshealth.org/parent/positive/family/net_safety.html
and *xblock.isafe.org/*

15

Obsession, compulsion, and addiction

What's wrong with being dedicated? Isn't it a good thing to try hard?

What's the difference between trying hard, compulsive behavior, and addiction?

Is there something you enjoy doing more than anything else? A keen interest in an activity can take up a large part of your life. This makes you happy because you enjoy doing it. But make sure that you leave room in your life for a range of other things as well.

An **obsession** is a persistent feeling or idea that a person cannot escape. The obsession is the actual feeling or the thought itself.

Some people are obsessed with making lots of money. They spend a large amount of their time thinking about ways to achieve this. Some people are obsessed with their weight. They are constantly thinking about how they can lose weight.

A **compulsion** is an uncontrollable urge to carry out a given act. While an obsession is a thought or feeling, a compulsion is an action—the action of continuing a pleasurable or repetitive activity. For example, a person obsessed with losing weight may start a compulsive behavior such as exercising much more than is healthy. The obsession drives the compulsion.

An addiction is when someone becomes psychologically or physically **dependent** on some habit, practice, or substance. The person might feel they cannot do without the thing they are addicted to. A gambler can become addicted to gambling; a person trying to lose weight can become addicted to diet pills.

Bec: Gran, Mom worries about everything. Switches are checked ten times before we leave the house. She triple checks the door locks. She doesn't seem to be able to stop. What's wrong with her?
Gran: Bec, your mother has been obsessed about worrying what things will go wrong for as long as I remember. Because of her **obsessive** worrying, she has developed a compulsive behavior. She just can't help herself. Just be patient with her. What if we discuss this with her doctor and see what else we can do?

Sam's diary

July 1

I always feel that I am left out at parties. Other people seem to have more friends, make more jokes, be the life of the party. Me, I'm just a bore at parties, with no friends.

July 7

A guy in our class, Jamie, gave me this pill at a birthday party last night. I felt so great! I was dancing with everyone. I even danced on the table. The other guys said I was the life of the party. I even got invited to another party next weekend by Rachel. I can't believe it!

July 14

What a night! I was a blast at Rachel's party. I started slow but luckily Jamie was there with more of those wonder pills. All my new friends loved me!

July 20

I have been invited to another exciting party at Aninja's place. But I couldn't find Jamie anywhere around school. I called his house. His mom says he is away. I cannot go the party without those pills. How will I make my new friends like being with me?

July 21

Left early from the party. I was not in the mood. Everyone was asking me what was wrong. It was terrible. I need to find Jamie before next weekend!

What happened to Sam? Did his obsession with having no friends turn into an addiction? What other problems could Sam face in the future?

About addiction

Most of us have hobbies and interests that are very important to us and that we like to spend time on. But if these interests become the only thing we talk about or care about, the behavior can be called obsessive. The next step can be addiction.

What is addiction?

Addiction is when a person feels they;

- MUST have or do a certain thing all the time;
- can only think about one thing;
- can't stop something, even if they want to or try to;
- can't control some part of their life.

Addiction does more than interfere with the way someone lives. It takes over their life.

What can people be addicted to?

People can become addicted to a wide range of things, such as:

- using the Internet
- drugs
- tobacco/smoking
- working
- undereating
- alcohol
- gambling
- collecting items
- exercise
- shopping
- some medications
- eating

They can't think of anything else. It is their first priority.

What is an addict?

Using drugs when you are not sick is called substance **abuse**. The drug is the substance, and it is not being used for a medical purpose. It is being abused. So is the person's body and mind.

Someone with a habit they cannot control is called an addict. The term "addict" commonly refers to someone whose habit is taking drugs.

Often people start taking drugs just to see how it feels—for a thrill. They might start off experimenting with drugs but end up addicted. Their habit can ruin their lives. It can even end in death.

Types of addiction

<u>Physical addiction</u> is when a body cannot manage without something. Addicts feel the need for more of the substance to be able to cope with life. When they try to give up the habit, their bodies react, making them feel sick and miserable. They experience things like hot and cold sweats, headaches, vomiting, and muscle pain.

These horrible feelings are called withdrawal **symptoms**. Addicts often want to go back to their habit rather than suffer the withdrawal symptoms. It is very hard to give up a physical addiction, but it is not impossible. Over time, withdrawal symptoms become less severe as the body gets used to coping without the substance.

<u>Emotional addiction</u> is when someone does not like the way they feel and thinks having a certain thing will change that. They might feel anxious or angry or sad if they don't get what they want.

Look back at the list of things people can be addicted to. See if you can work out what type of addiction each one is.

Media and risk

Whether you like it or not, what you watch on TV, see in newspapers and on posters, and hear on the radio can influence what you think. That influence can be positive or negative.

KIDS ARE FAST LEARNE

No parent wants their child to become addicted to cigarettes. Cigarette smoke contains over 4,000 c... It's a toxic, poisonous mix of substances. So it's no surprise smoking causes death and disease. Whe... there's less chance their child will grow up to be a smoker and more chance they'll have a full and he...

Media has a **positive influence** when it helps to reduce risk. You may have seen advertisements from an organization called Truth. Their anti-smoking campaign shows people the negative effects of using tobacco products. Similarly, the Ad Council has used media sources to promote positive social messages for years. You may have seen their commercials against drinking and driving.

Media has a negative influence when people behaving badly—getting drunk, smoking, stealing, fighting, damaging property, and breaking laws—are presented as cool. Making unhealthy risks look attractive can encourage people to copy the risky behavior.

This event is drug and alcohol free!

So does "drug and alcohol free" mean the drugs are given out for free? Of course not. It's like a dog-free park. It means they're banned. When concerts, parties, or celebrations are drug free, it makes them safer places for people under 18 to have fun.

Have you ever been to a First Night Celebration? Dozens of cities around the United States have First Night Celebrations on New Years Eve every year. The event was started in Boston, Massachusetts, in 1976. The founders wanted to give artists and families an entertaining, safe way to celebrate the New Year. Since then, it has spread to cities across the United States. First Night Celebrations offer a drug- and alcohol-free atmosphere that promotes community, creativity, and cultural diversity. They are also a lot of fun! To find out more, visit www.firstnight.com.

21   ▶21A   21

Are alternative therapies risky?

Have you ever sipped hot lemon with honey when you've had a sore throat, rubbed clove oil on an aching tooth, or taken vitamins? For thousands of years, people have used nonmedical ways to cure sickness or pain and stay well. These are often called **alternative** medicines or **therapies**.

Examples of alternative therapies:

- acupuncture: a technique in which very thin needles of varying lengths are inserted into the skin at certain spots to treat a variety of conditions

- aromatherapy: using fragrant oils made from plants to alter mood or improve health

- massage therapy: rubbing and pushing on muscles and body tissue to relieve muscle tension and pain

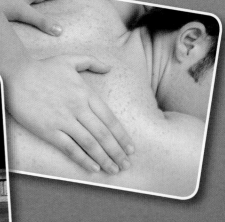

Pharmacies and supermarkets sell all kinds of medicines to deal with minor sickness and health problems, such as headaches and stress. Sometimes medicine is necessary, but sometimes it is not. You might just need to blow the cobwebs out of your head with fresh air and exercise or take time to relax. Listening to music, going for a walk, doing some artwork, digging in the garden—all sorts of risk-free, drug-free activities can improve the way you feel.

Some alternative therapies that are good for relaxation are:

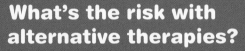

- meditation—a kind of concentration to relax the body and calm the mind;

- yoga—an ancient Hindu form of exercise that involves special body movements and deep breathing to strengthen muscles and relax the mind;

- Tai Chi—an ancient Chinese martial art that uses movement, meditation, and controlled breathing to improve well-being.

What's the risk with alternative therapies?

Whether there is a risk or not will depend on each individual's physical and emotional health. If you are not sure, check with your doctor.

Alternative medicines (even natural ones) can interact with prescription medicines to make them less safe. Always tell your doctor about any alternative medicines you are taking.

The government has strict rules about alternative medicines to help protect you, but there can be risks if alternative **therapists** are not well trained. Remember, they are not usually doctors. Do some homework. Ask if you can talk to other customers who have used the treatment. Carefully read the information the therapist has available. Be sure it is useful for your condition. Alternative medicines should not be used instead of something your doctor has prescribed.

Gambling with your life

Gambling is taking a RISK, and sometimes that is an adventurous thing to do.

Trying a new sport where you are a bit scared, venturing into a new place, or starting new friendships are all types of risks. There are good risks, which make us try adventures, and bad risks, which can be foolish.

Gambling is a dangerous risk if it gets out of control and becomes compulsive behavior. If the odds of being seriously hurt, causing damage to others, or destroying things is high, then the gamble is stupid, not adventurous.

Taking on dares to do dangerous things—where the odds of getting seriously hurt are high—is gambling with death. Some examples are:

- riding a bike without a helmet;
- driving without a license;
- getting into a car when you know the driver has been drinking;
- climbing to or jumping from dangerous places;
- carrying a weapon;
- drinking alcohol to the point of vomiting or blacking out;
- getting into a fight.

9 ♥

Check your own dangerous risk taking with these questions:

- If someone dares you to do something, do you always do it?
- Before you start something physically dangerous, do you ever think what might happen if you got injured for life?
- Have you ever gambled with your life in any way?
- Do you bet?
- Do you prefer to use other words than "gambling with your life" to describe what you do?
- Do you get a buzz from doing something that is banned or against the rules?
- Do you ever regret doing something risky?

7 ♦

Sometimes it's exciting and challenging to take a risk—a positive risk. A safe bet is when you act only after you have thought carefully and taken steps to make sure there is no real danger. For example, extreme sports professionals will not try a new trick on a snowboard or jump with a BMX until they've trained, practiced, and have a safety plan in place. A safe bet is a smart bet!

2 ♣

Taking risks is not a bad habit, but taking risks without considering the consequences can lead to injury: yours and others.

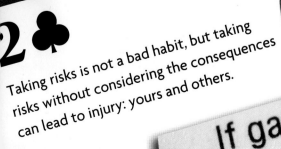

If gambling is a problem for someone you know, call t

How can people help?

What can people do if someone has been drugged or poisoned?

Get help!

Do you remember the number for the Poison Control Center? Do you know where to find the number for your family doctor? What about the ambulance service? Has someone in your family completed a first-aid course? Do you know where to find the school nurse at your school?

If conscious:

- find out what kind of poison or drug was taken;
- call for medical help;
- keep the person calm;
- do not try to make them vomit, as different poisons have different treatments.

If the person is unconscious:

- do not move the person;
- call for medical help;
- listen and look for signs of breathing;
- get someone who is trained to use **resuscitation** methods;
- look for clues about what the poison is.

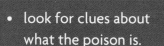

Dial 911

If you are at the scene of an emergency, you need to call for help immediately. Dial 911 to reach Emergency Services. The person who answers your call can send the ambulance and fire or police services if they are needed. It is likely that you will be nervous and upset when you call, but you will be most helpful if you stay calm. Follow these instructions:

- speak clearly and do not hang up;
- explain what type of emergency it is;

How can you recognize a person needing help with an addiction?

If someone you care about is showing several of these signs, then they could be suffering from an addiction and need help:

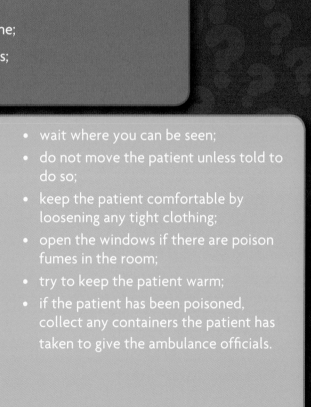

- moods swings;
- seeming to drop out of life among family and friends;
- showing no interest in something that used to be a big interest;
- getting behind in school or work;
- avoiding friends or hanging out with others who use drugs;
- selling their stuff or stealing yours;
- acting upset, anxious, or really down;
- not sleeping or sleeping most of the time;
- changing their eating times and patterns;
- losing or gaining weight quickly.

- be ready to give information about exactly where you are and what phone number you are calling from;
- say whether the injured or sick person (the patient) is conscious or not;
- say whether you are alone with the patient or if there is an adult present.

While you are waiting for the ambulance:
- make sure doors and gates are unlocked if necessary;
- turn on the lights at night;
- wait where you can be seen;
- do not move the patient unless told to do so;
- keep the patient comfortable by loosening any tight clothing;
- open the windows if there are poison fumes in the room;
- try to keep the patient warm;
- if the patient has been poisoned, collect any containers the patient has taken to give the ambulance officials.

The SAFEST way to help is to get medical advice. Talk to a doctor, school nurse, counselor, or any adult you can trust.

What's the problem?

Sometimes sharing our problems can help others, too, like in this talkback radio session.

Presenter: Welcome to Community Radio's health program for kids. Dr. Strong will answer your calls. Welcome, Dr. Strong.

Dr. Strong: Thank you once again. It's always good to talk to your listeners. Let's see who's on the line.

Caller 1: I'm a diabetic so I have to have shots and watch what I eat. What should I do when other kids tease me about having a **syringe**?

Dr. Strong: Do they understand why? Ask the teacher if you can give a talk about what a diabetic has to do to stay healthy. Or see if the hospital has a diabetes educator who could come and talk to the school. That will help!

Presenter: Our next caller is really into sports. What's your question, caller 2?

Caller 2: I tore a muscle and the doctor gave me these pills to help it heal. It is taking ages to get better. What would happen if I took more than the doctor prescribed? Would I get better faster?

Dr. Strong: No. More is not better. It may make you sick and even harm your recovery.

Presenter: It seems we have a number of boys interested in sports today. Hi, caller 3, what's your question for Dr. Strong?

Caller 3: I hate wearing a mouthguard because I can't breathe properly when I run, but Coach insists on it. Why bother?

Dr. Strong: Mouthguards can be a little uncomfortable at first, but there are good reasons why they are essential. A major one is there is less pain if you get hit in the face! Mouthguards protect your teeth and jaw. They can even help prevent you from getting knocked out in a serious clash. That's all much more important than comfort! Who's next?

Caller 4: Hi, Dr. Strong. I'm Beth and my problem is my mom. Sometimes she drinks and she forgets about picking me up from school and stuff. She cries a lot or gets really angry with me, but I'm not sure what I've done wrong. I love my mom and I've tried looking for help on the Internet, but I don't know where to start.

Dr. Strong: Good for you, Beth, for having the courage to speak up. It sounds to me like you and your mom both need help. I can certainly give you an idea where to start. Grab a pencil, Beth, and take down this phone number. You can call the Girls and Boys Town National Hotline for free at any time. Someone is always there to talk to you about what you can do. All our callers should look up that number.

Presenter: I'd like to add, for Beth and others like her, that you will find a great deal of information out there on the Internet but it's not all good. And it's certainly not all suitable for young people. So places we can all trust, like the Girls and Boys Town National Hotline, are an important part of a healthy community.

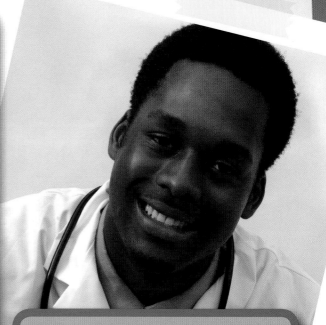

Now, we have another serious problem here, Dr. Strong. A couple of callers want to talk about drugs. Go ahead, caller 5.

Caller 5: If I know other kids at school have illegal drugs, what should I do?

Dr. Strong: Talk with the school **counselor** or your principal. This is not tattling, and it may save a life.

Caller 6: What do I do or say if somebody offers me drugs?

Dr. Strong: Say no! Again, talk with the school counselor, your parents, or your principal. Never let anyone talk you into experimenting with drugs.

Presenter: That's good advice to end with. Thank you, Dr. Strong, for speaking with our callers today. I'm sure you've helped lots of listeners. And to our callers, thank you for sharing. Be sure to tune in again next week.

Toward a healthy balance

Other people can't make you take risks.

Other people can't make you feel obsessive.

Be the boss of your feelings.

If someone you know or care about is involved in risky business:

- talk to them about the problem;
- remind them about their good points and how important they are;
- explain that their risky behavior affects others, too;
- remember to look after yourself;
- tell an adult you trust about the problem;
- find out more about the problem to help you understand;
- think about whether it is wise for you to hang around with that person;
- suggest they see the school counselor;
- never be tempted to try the same thing.

Saying NO can be cool, too.

Glossary

abuse	use in a bad or wrong way
addicted	feeling like one must have something all the time
alternative	another way; different choice
antiseptic	a substance that keeps germs from growing
compulsion	an uncontrollable need to perform an act
conscious	awake; knowing what is happening around you
counselor	professional advisor who listens to your worries
dependent	relying on or needing something or someone for support
dispense	give out medicine
first aid	treatment given to a sick or hurt person before they can get to a doctor
obsession	activity or idea that takes up all of someone's time and energy
obsessive	doing something all the time that is not sensible or reasonable
pharmacist	person who makes up and gives out medicines
pharmacy	shop selling drugs and medicines
prescribe	when a medical doctor grants permission to buy a special medicine
resuscitation	the reviving of someone, usually after they are unconscious
symptom	the way a body reacts or changes because of a disease or injury
syringe	a needle for putting medicine into the body
therapist	someone who performs a treatment to make the body well
therapy	treatment to cure illness or make the body well
unconscious	not aware of what is going on; not awake or thinking
well-being	good health

For Further Information

Books

Ballard, Carol. *Safety and Risk Taking*. Farmington Hills, MI: Gale, 2004.

Spilsbury, Louise. *Be Smart, Stay Safe!* Chicago, IL: Heinemann Library, 2009.

Web Sites

Internet Safety

www.netsmartz.org

Mayo Clinic: First Aid

www.mayoclinic.com/health/FirstAidIndex/FirstAidIndex

Publisher's note to educators and parents: Our editors have carefully reviewed these Web sites to ensure that they are suitable for students. Many Web sites change frequently, however, and we cannot guarantee that a site's future contents will continue to meet our high standards of quality and educational value. Be advised that students should be closely supervised whenever they access the Internet.

Index